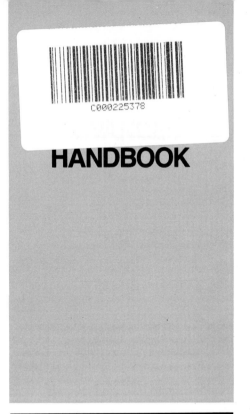

C000225378

HANDBOOK

G12/93

Published by the
ROYAL YACHTING ASSOCIATION
RYA House, Romsey Road, Eastleigh
Hampshire SO50 9YA

© 1993 Royal Yachting Association

Throughout this book the pronouns 'he', 'him'
and 'his' have been used inclusively and are
intended to apply to both men and women. It is
important in sport as elsewhere that women and
men should have equal status and equal
opportunities.

Cover photo of Laser 2 by courtesy of the
Laser Centre

Illustrations by Maxine Kirk
and Jo Mooring-Aldridge

The aim of this booklet is to provide a concise summary of the essential techniques and background knowledge required for the RYA National Dinghy Certificate, Levels 3 and 5.

It is not a substitute for a practical course of instruction at an RYA recognised teaching establishment, but should be used as background reading before your course, as a reminder of essential points during the course and for revision after you have completed the certificate requirements.

As far as possible, the text follows the syllabus headings given in the RYA Dinghy Sailing Logbook G4. As some of the content of the Advanced Skills course – Level 5 is a refinement of the principles outlined at Level 3, it is appropriate to group the content by subject, rather than by Level. To avoid confusion, items specifically related to Level 5 are identified by a different page tone.

RYA dinghy courses are taught at hundreds of RYA recognised centres around Britain and inevitably there will be minor variations in instructional techniques and emphasis. Do not be concerned if you are taught slight differences on the techniques outlined below.

What is important is that you should understand what you are trying to achieve and how to sail your dinghy to best advantage. Much of this booklet is concerned with boat handling manoeuvres, to which a single principle may be applied.

Rather than simply follow instructions, first consider what you are trying to achieve. Each exercise can be split into four parts – planning, approach, manoeuvre, escape. Before starting any exercise or manoeuvre, think through each of those elements.

Some of the background information for the dinghy courses is already contained in other RYA publications. Important details have been reprinted here but you are referred to the appropriate booklet, many of which are free to RYA members. Similarly, when a topic deserves more attention than is possible in this booklet, a recommendation for further reading is given in the Bibliography.

Two of the Level 5 topics are not included here, because it is impossible to cover them adequately in the space available. It would be possible to sketch out the detail of what should be covered in First Aid and Boat Construction/Repair, but that would merely repeat the syllabus given in the Logbook G4. Instead, reference is made to some excellent books on the subject in the Bibliography.

Improving Techniques – Level 3 Course

The RYA Level 3 course is not for beginners. When you start a Level 3 course, it is assumed that you hold the National Dinghy Certificate – Level 2 or that you have the practical skills and theoretical knowledge of that award.

In other words, you should be able to rig, launch, sail around a triangular course and return safely in light weather conditions. The aim of the Level 3 course is to improve those basic sailing techniques and provide more background knowledge. By the end of the course you will have a competent, safe, practical approach to sailing in moderate conditions and you will make sound, sensible decisions.

Advanced Skills – Level 5 Course

Before considering a Level 5 course, you should have mastered the techniques and absorbed the background knowledge of Level 3. In practical terms, this implies a season's sailing between courses. You need not, however, have completed a Racing Techniques course; indeed many advanced sailors have little interest in this aspect of the sport.

The aim of this course is to refine personal sailing skills and background theoretical knowledge to the point where you will have a confident, safe approach to sailing and be capable of handling almost any dinghy in strong winds. In addition, you should be ready to contemplate day sailing passages in open sea conditions without safety cover – the world of dinghy cruising.

RIGGING

By the end of an RYA Level 3 course, you should be capable of rigging a wide variety of dinghies. Although individual details vary, the general principles remain the same, including the use of halyard and clew outhaul tension to change the fullness of the mainsail. By the time you reach Level 5, your knowledge will include the effect of rig controls such as mast blocks to govern rig geometry before you go afloat, and the effect of changes in sheeting position, kicking strap tension and other sail controls whilst afloat. It should also cover the rigging of spinnaker equipment and ideally preparation for trapeze work.

Sheet bend

Used for joining two ropes together. Make the loop in the thicker rope and then make the knot as shown. It is stronger with an extra turn around the loop, when it is known as a double sheet bend. Undo by holding the ropes on both sides of the knot and pushing your hands towards each other.

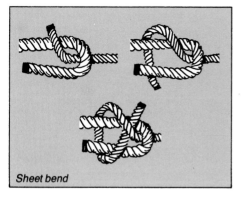

Sheet bend

Clove hitch

Useful for securing a rope to a spar, or for attaching a burgee stick to its halyard. It can be difficult to undo when wet.

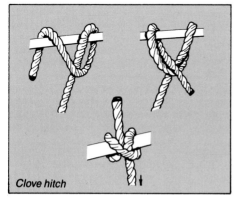

Clove hitch

Heat Sealing

The ends of most modern ropes can be heat sealed to prevent them fraying or unlaying. Effectively this means melting the man-made fibres together with a "hot-knife", gas flame or match.

Fisherman's bend

A more secure alternative to the round turn and two half hitches; the end is taken through the turns before the half hitches are made.

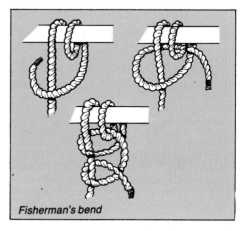

Fisherman's bend

Rolling hitch

The most secure way of attaching a rope to a spar or another rope, where both will be under tension. Sailing schools and clubs occasionally stream a long towing line behind the safety boat; this hitch should be used to secure your dinghy to that line.

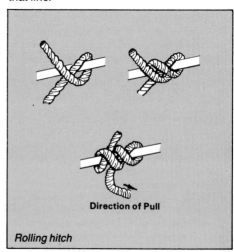

Direction of Pull

Rolling hitch

Common whipping

Lay a loop of twine along the rope then wind turns around tightly for about 20mm. Put the end through the loop, pull the protruding thread and cut off the loose ends.

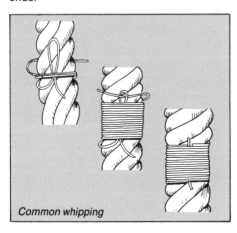

Common whipping

Eye splice

Unlay about 100mm of the rope and make a temporary seizing. Form an eye and tuck the strands under the standing part in the order shown. The only tricky part is where the third strand is inserted – turn the rope over to get it right. A minimum of three tucks of each strand is needed for security, then the strands can be tapered before making further tucks to get a neat finish.

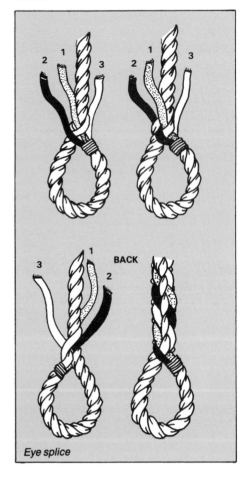

Eye splice

The majority of damage to sailing dinghies is caused when they are being launched and recovered. Take care to ensure that the hull does not come into contact with the beach. That means at least one member of the crew must be prepared to get wet. Thorough preparation of the boat before launching is essential.

The sails should be bent on, sheets led correctly without twists or tangles and the boat securely attached to the trolley with a suitable quick release knot. All the gear should be checked before going near the water. In particular, ensure that buoyancy tank hatches and bungs are secure, that the anchor, paddle(s) and bucket are attached and that the rudder and tiller are ready to use.

Launching from a windward shore

The boat should be trolleyed to the edge of the water and the sails hoisted with the boat head to wind. If the onshore waves are small or moderate, the boat can be pushed into the water and floated off the trolley still head to wind. If the wind is not blowing directly off the shore, you might prefer to launch before hoisting the sails.

In larger waves, the boat may rise with a wave then drop onto its trolley, damaging the hull. If there is any danger of this, the boat should be carried into the water (this may mean organising a team of helpers).

Leaving a beach with an offshore wind is straightforward. The boat is held into the wind by the crew while the helmsman gets aboard and prepares the rudder and tiller and overhauls the mainsheet so that the mainsail can be freed right off.

The crew pushes the bow off in the preferred direction and climbs in on the windward side of the boat, backing the jib if necessary to help the dinghy bear away. When the water is deep enough the rudder is pulled right down and the centreboard adjusted to suit the point of sailing.

The procedure for leaving a jetty on a windward shore is similar, except that both helmsman and crew may board and rig the

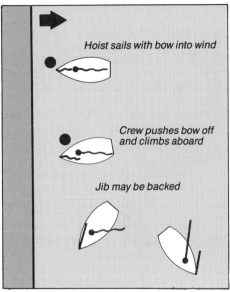

Hoist sails with bow into wind

Crew pushes bow off and climbs aboard

Jib may be backed

Leaving a windward shore

boat, having first secured the painter with a slip knot. When ready, the crew can push off from the jetty, slip the painter and back the jib as before.

In congested areas it may be necessary to leave the beach or jetty by sailing backwards. Properly done, this technique appears elegant, but it is not simply a matter of pushing the boom as far forward as you can and holding it in position.

There are three important points to remember:

★ Concentrate crew weight well forward in the boat. This lifts the stern clear of the water, reducing drag and making steering easier. Don't forget to raise the centreboard, as it is not needed to prevent leeway and its presence will exaggerate course corrections.

★ Keep a firm hand on the tiller. The rudder is effectively at the front of the boat and as you gather speed the water pressure on either side of it is large. Only very small tiller movements are needed to control your course; remember that the

rudder is operating in reverse.
★ When you have sailed backwards far
  enough, choose which way you want
  the dinghy to be heading to sail off.
  Unless hazards restrict the choice, it
  is easier to get out of this manoeuvre
  by pointing the tiller towards the
  boom. That way, the boat will turn
  and the mainsail will end up to
  leeward without the boom having first
  swung right across the boat in an
  inadvertent gybe.

Returning to a windward shore

Landing on a windward shore is again
relatively simple, as long as one member of
the crew accepts that he may get wet.
  ★ Pick a suitable spot. If you don't know
    the area and didn't take local advice
    about underwater hazards or rocks
    before launching, look around
    carefully and try to assess where
    hazards are likely.
  ★ Sail to a position where the landing
    site can be reached on a close reach,
    allowing for the extra leeway which
    will be made as the centreboard is
    raised in shallow water. Sail towards
    the shore and ease sheets to slow
    down. Let fly the jib and raise
    centreboard and rudder as
    necessary.
  ★ As you make the final approach, ease
    the mainsheet. The crew should be

ready to slip over the windward side
at the right moment to hold the boat
head to wind while the helmsman
lowers and secures the sails, raises
the centreboard fully and removes
the rudder.

Launching from a lee shore

In strong winds and exposed
beaches, the more help which can be found
to launch from a lee shore, the better.
Substantial damage can be caused by the
boat either being dropped by a wave onto
its trolley or onto the beach. A number of
people lifting the boat from its trolley into
deep water will eliminate the risk, but this
kind of help cannot always be found.

If not, choose a favourable site. It may
be possible to move the boat into the lee of
a harbour wall or a breakwater. You may be
able to take advantage of a change in the
shape of the shore so that the wind is not
blowing directly onshore. Assess the wave
pattern and choose the best tack on which
to leave the shore; it is better to get through
the waves at right angles.

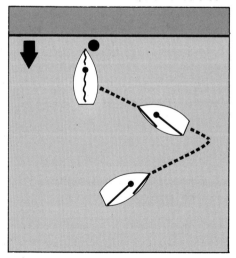

Returning to a windward shore

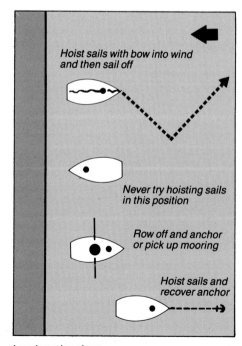

Leaving a lee shore

Wheel the boat bow first into the water, having first secured the bow to the trolley with only a round turn or a slip knot. Float the boat on a suitable wave and pull it clear of the trolley as quickly as possible. Retrieve the trolley then, with the crew holding the boat head to wind in water deep enough to prevent the stern grounding in the wave troughs, the helmsman hoists the sails, attaches the rudder and lowers the centreboard as far as possible.

The helmsman sheets in the mainsail and the crew pushes the bow in the right direction and climbs in on the windward side of the boat. As the boat reaches deeper water the crew can lower the centreboard and trim the jib, whilst the helmsman lowers the rudder fully.

Alternative methods

It may pay to row or paddle the boat off a lee shore, particularly if the dinghy can be rowed to a mooring before the sails are hoisted.

At some clubs and centres lines are trailed ashore from buoys or anchors. The boat can be hauled clear of the shore before the sails are set. Such lines are most often seen at centres operating in areas of strong tidal streams or large ranges, as they also allow several boats to be left afloat for some time.

Returning to a lee shore

The easiest way to land on a lee shore is to turn the boat head to wind some way off,

drop the mainsail and come in under jib alone.

★ The helmsman turns the boat into the wind
★ The crew lowers the mainsail and raises the centreboard
★ The helmsman bears away, sailing under jib alone
★ The helmsman lifts the rudder blade a little, or prepares to do so, if he knows the beach is steep-to
★ When in shallow water, the crew lets the jib fly and jumps into the water and turns the boat head to wind
★ The helmsman lowers the jib and removes the rudder.

With practice, the alternative is for the helmsman to head for the shore under full sail, rounding up at the last minute to allow the crew to jump out and hold the boat. The helmsman then lowers the mainsail, removes the rudder and the lowers the jib. For obvious reasons, this technique is not recommended on unknown beaches.

On exposed beaches with large waves neither of these techniques is possible, because of the danger of the boat being rolled over in the surf. The only safe way to lad is to sail straight for the shore at full speed, with centreboard up, crew weight right aft and the helmsman ready to raise the rudder blade at the last moment. This technique, common at some coastal clubs in parts of the UK, relies on having a gang of helpers ready to lift the boat clear of the water immediately upon landing.

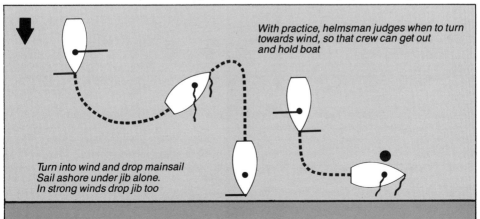

With practice, helmsman judges when to turn towards wind, so that crew can get out and hold boat

Turn into wind and drop mainsail
Sail ashore under jib alone.
In strong winds drop jib too

Landing on a lee shore

Landing and re-launching

If you want to land on a lee shore and then sail off again after a short break, the following variation may be useful. Success depends on knowing the length of your anchor warp and assessing distances accurately.

* ★ Sail towards the lee shore, turn head to wind and drop anchor
* ★ Raise centreboard and remove rudder; in strong winds, lower sails at this stage
* ★ Pay out anchor warp to allow boat to drift towards shore until close enough for crew to jump out; if sails had been left hoisted to aid drift, they should be lowered now
* ★ Depending on wave conditions, either carry dinghy ashore or haul off into slightly deeper water to avoid damage

To sail away, simply haul on the anchor warp until you are in deep water, hoist sails, recover anchor and sail away.

If you are blown aground on a lee shore unintentionally and cannot sail off again immediately, lower your sails. Do not raise the centreboard, because you will only be blown further on. To get afloat again, try rowing, paddling or kedging off.

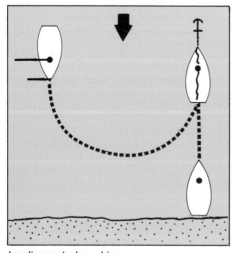

Landing and relaunching

Moorings

Picking up and leaving moorings in tidal waters is a relatively simple process – just as long as you take the tidal stream into account. Assess the effect of the tide by looking at boats on swinging moorings or looking at the flow of water past objects fixed to the seabed.

There are basically two techniques for picking up or leaving moorings on tidal waters, depending on whether wind and tide are in the same direction or opposed. In either case, you must choose a route to or from the buoy which takes account of tidal stream, amount of sail set and any hazards. Remember that light sailing dinghies will usually be wind-rode rather than tide-rode, except in light winds and strong tidal conditions.

Approaching a mooring – wind and tide together

* ★ Assess direction of wind and tide
* ★ Choose a close-hauled or close reach course to the buoy
* ★ Prepare the boat's mooring line, leading it through the bow fairlead if appropriate
* ★ Let the jib fly
* ★ Ease the mainsail to reduce speed so that it stops with the buoy at the windward shroud
* ★ Secure the mooring line
* ★ Lower sails, raise centreboard and remove rudder.

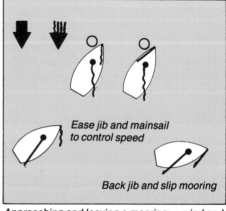

Ease jib and mainsail to control speed

Back jib and slip mooring

Approaching and leaving a mooring – wind and tide together

Leaving a mooring – wind and tide together

★ Assess direction of wind and tide
★ Prepare mooring line for slipping
★ Hoist sails, attach rudder and lower centreboard
★ Back the jib, slip the mooring line and sail away.

Approaching a mooring – wind and tide opposed

★ Assess direction of wind and tide
★ Sail upwind of the mooring buoy, turn head to wind, lower mainsail and raise centreboard
★ Prepare the boat's mooring line
★ Sail back towards the mooring buoy under jib alone
★ On reaching the buoy, let the jib fly and secure the mooring line
★ Lower jib and remove rudder.

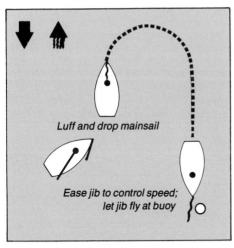

Luff and drop mainsail

Ease jib to control speed; let jib fly at buoy

Approaching a mooring – wind and tide opposed

Leaving a mooring – wind and tide opposed

★ Assess direction of wind and tide
★ Hoist jib and attach rudder
★ Slip mooring line and sheet in jib
★ Sail to an area with plenty of searoom and let jib fly
★ Push helm hard away and hoist mainsail.

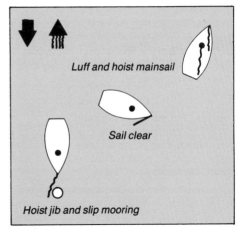

Luff and hoist mainsail

Sail clear

Hoist jib and slip mooring

Leaving a mooring – wind and tide opposed

Making fast to buoys

Unless your dinghy is kept on a mooring, it is likely that you will only be securing to mooring buoys as a temporary measure. Conventionally, you will make your painter fast using a round turn and two half hitches through the ring of the buoy, or through the mooring strop secured to the chain riser underneath the buoy. Alternatively, pass your painter through the ring or strop and bring it back on aboard to be secured around the heel of the mast. This method makes leaving the mooring a simple operation.

Coming alongside a moored yacht, jetty or pontoon

The procedure is very similar to picking up a mooring. The most important preliminary is to establish the direction of wind and tide. Once again, there are basically two procedures, with a third slight variation.

When wind and tide are in similar or opposite directions, follow the routines outlined above for picking up a mooring. The only additional problem is that with jetties or pontoons your choice of escape routes is likely to be more limited if things go wrong with the approach.

The third variation is if the wind is blowing across the tide. The principle to remember is that when the sails are hoisted the dinghy is likely to be wind-rode; when they are dropped it is likely to be tide-rode.

11

This will not apply when one of the forces is much stronger than the other but it makes a good general rule.

Your approach should always be into the tide. If the jetty or pontoon lies parallel to the tide, choose which side of it to approach.

If you are heading for the leeward side of the jetty, treat it as 'wind and tide together' and approach with both sails up. If you have to sail for the windward side of the jetty, treat it as 'wind and tide opposed' and lower the mainsail.

If the jetty or pontoon is perpendicular to the tide, always head for the downtide side. Treat it as 'wind and tide together' and do not lower the sails until your mooring line is secure.

Making fast alongside

Although with a lightweight dinghy you can make fast with just bow and stern lines, the following method provides security for all sizes of craft.

Normally four ropes are used to secure a boat alongside. The head rope is led from the bow well forward along the jetty. Similarly the stern rope is led aft from the stern. These are normally the first two ropes taken ashore, since they will locate the boat in her berth.

Better security is provided by springs, which hold bow and stern in to the jetty and prevent the boat from surging alongside. One spring is taken from the bow to a point aft. This is known as the forward spring because it stops the boat moving forward. The back spring or after spring is taken from the boat's stern to a point well forward.

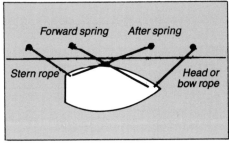

Mooring alongside

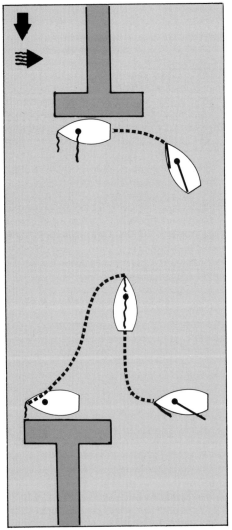

Approaching a jetty – wind across tide

Anchoring

Although there are several different types of anchor, you will find that the type most often used at sailing centres is the CQR or plough anchor. The differences in design cater for different seabeds or stowage requirements, but the CQR represents a good compromise for dinghy sailing.

A short length of chain attached to the anchor serves two purposes. Its weight ensures that the pull from the anchor warp is as nearly horizontal as possible, so helping the anchor to dig into the seabed. In addition, it protects the warp from chafe on the seabed.

Attached to the chain is the anchor warp, which must be strong enough to hold the weight of dinghy being anchored and long enough to suit the area of your sailing. In order to get an efficient pull on the anchor, the 'rule of thumb' when using warp is to pay out a length which is five times the depth of water.

The bitter end of the warp should be attached to the boat at a suitable strong point, the favourite one being the heel of the mast. Because the anchor may be needed quickly, it must be stowed for instant use in such a way that it can be run out freely. The usual options are to coil it in a bucket or on a drum or to make up a coil which is secured with a buntline hitch.

Although the bitter end of the anchor warp is firmly secured, you may want to ensure that the warp runs out over the bow of the dinghy when lying at anchor. If your boat does not have a bow fairlead, you can improvise with a loop of line tied to the stemhead fitting.

Selecting an anchorage

When choosing a spot to anchor, consider the following:
★ Are there any underwater obstructions?
★ Will your anchor hold in the seabed?
★ What is the depth of water?
★ How close are other water users, main channels etc? Will you swing into them?
★ What is the expected tidal range?

Methods of anchoring

Just as when approaching a mooring, you must take wind and tide into account. Sailing dinghies tend to be more wind-rode than tide-rode, except in strong tides and light winds.

When wind and tide are in similar directions:
★ Approach the chosen site on a close reach
★ Prepare the anchor and warp, leading the latter forward under the jibsheet and through the bow fairlead
★ Slow down by easing sheets to stop upwind/uptide of where you want to lie
★ When the boat has stopped, let the anchor go as the boat starts to drift backwards, then pay òut chain and warp smoothly
★ When enough warp has been run out, secure the warp and check that the anchor is holding by reference to stationary objects (i.e. take a transit)
★ Raise the centreboard and lower the sails.

When wind and tide are opposed, and you expect the dinghy to be tide-rode:
★ Choose your site and sail upwind from it
★ Prepare anchor and warp
★ Sail head to wind and lower your mainsail
★ Sail downwind under jib alone
★ Ease the jib as you approach the chosen spot
★ Let the jib fly and lower the anchor
★ Pay out warp, then secure and check anchor is holding
★ Lower jib.

Clearing a fouled anchor

The most common reason for fouling a dinghy anchor is if you have anchored in an area where mooring chains are lying on the seabed. Alternatively, the anchor may be fouled on a rock and a conventional straight pull will not shift it.

The way to clear it is to pull on the anchor from a different angle. If you cannot clear it by sailing around and pulling on the warp so that the pull comes on the anchor from a different direction, try dropping another line down to the anchor itself.

Do this by tying a loop of line around your anchor warp, weight it with something suitable and allow it to drop down the warp. Then take the strain on this line rather than on the anchor warp and try sailing around the anchor and pulling on this line.

Heaving to

In the RYA Level 1 course we use the term 'basic hove-to position' to describe how a dinghy lies when the sheets are freed and the tiller released. Strictly speaking, this is merely 'lying-to' and has the disadvantages that both sails are flapping noisily and the boat is drifting quickly downwind.

The proper 'hove-to' position is with the jib backed, tiller secured to leeward and centreboard partially raised. The easiest way of getting into this position is to tack leaving the jibsheet cleated and then push the tiller to leeward.

The backed jib tries to make the boat bear away but as soon as it picks up any speed the rudder has the effect of luffing it up again. Thus the dinghy will remain almost at a constant angle to the wind, forereaching gently. As strictly

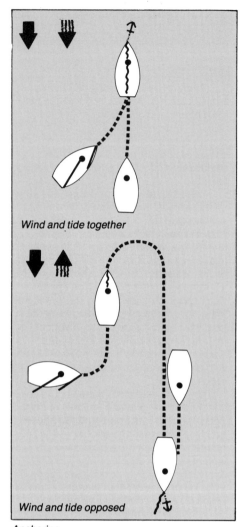

Wind and tide together

Wind and tide opposed

Anchoring

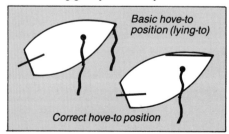

Basic hove-to position (lying-to)

Correct hove-to position

Heaving to

speaking you are underway and making way when hove-to, it is sensible to heave to on starboard tack unless you face the far more important consideration of heaving to on the tack which will take you away from the nearest danger.

Reefing afloat

The techniques of heaving to and reefing afloat come together in the RYA Dinghy Certificate because the first is a necessary prelude to the second.

Reefing is the technique of setting the right amount of sail for the weather conditions. It is always better to reef ashore before setting out; indeed in some ways you might think that reefing afloat is a sign of failure to predict the amount of sail needed.

There are, however, times when you need to reef afloat and the first step is to pick a suitable place to reef. If you can pick up a mooring or drop anchor, this may make the whole operation easier. If neither is possible, make sure that you have plenty of searoom to leeward so that the boat doesn't drift ashore or into danger while you are reefing.

Your goal when reefing should be a sail reduced by the required amount which still has an efficient shape, with no wrinkles. The boom should be level and the kicking strap should still be effective. With practice, you should be able to do the job in a boat equippped with roller reefing in about two minutes – much less if you have slab reefing.

★ Heave to on the favoured tack
★ Lower the mainsail by a third
★ Remove the kicking strap and bottom batten
★ Take a tuck of about 0.5m in the leech of the mainsail then roll the boom round and round, keeping tension on the clew
★ As you reef, roll a reefing strop or sailbag into the sail to take the place of the kicking strap attachment
★ Fit the boom back on the gooseneck and rehoist the mainsail
★ Re-attach the kicking strap and sail away.

Reefing a singlehander

It is much, much easier to reef a singlehander ashore than afloat. The most popular singlehanded dinghies (Laser, Topper) are reefed by rolling the sail around the mast, not around the boom. Some singlehanders may be reefed in the same way as two-man dinghies whilst others have no provision for reefing at all.

To reef a Laser or Topper afloat, first sail to a close reach position, free the tack downhaul or Cunningham, remove the kicking strap, ease the clew outhaul completely and (in the case of a Laser) take the boom off the gooseneck.

Rotate the mast in its step to roll the sail up. With a Laser you can only reef as far as the top batten (unless you've capsized the boat and removed it!); a Topper can be heavily reefed and still remain manoeuvrable. Having rolled up the sail, replace the boom, tack downhaul, outhaul and kicker and sail away.

Towing

A sailing dinghy which is being towed should have:
★ the sails lowered
★ the centreboard raised
★ the crew weight aft.

Failure to do this will cause the dinghy to sheer from one side to the other behind the towing vessel. In a normal tow, the tow line should always be through the bow fairlead of the dinghy being towed and attached to a suitable strong point. A couple of turns around the mast with a half hitch to finish is usually sufficient.

Passing a towline

In calm weather the two boats can simply lie alongside each other whilst the tow rope is passed across. If you have to tow one sailing dinghy with another in stronger winds, sail across the bows of the dinghy to be towed on a close-hauled course from the leeward quarter, passing the towline as you go. Sheets can be eased when the towline is made fast. Then bear away onto a reach to pick up speed.

In the case of a motor boat passing a line prior to towing a sailing boat, the line should be thrown from upwind of the dinghy.

Securing a towline

The strain of the towline must be transmitted over the whole boat and not an individual fitting, unless that fitting has been specifically designed for the purpose. In the absence of such a fitting, this usually means anchorage round the mast or a thwart.

Take a turn around the point of the towline's anchorage. This will take the strain off the end of the rope, will prevent damage and injury and will make things easier for you to secure the towline.

Take up the strain slowly to avoid damage by putting a shock load on the towline. Good communication between the two boats is vital; work out a simple set of signals.

Methods of towing

Towing one sailing dinghy with another, you will find that the difficulties come when you want to change direction, particularly if your course home is upwind. The longer the towline, the easier it is to tack without being stopped short by the snatch on the line as the towed boat changes course behind you. When towing in a tideway, do make extra allowance for the drift of the towed vessel when manoeuvring around buoys or other obstructions.

When towing with a powered craft, there are times when towing alongside is preferable to the conventional tow astern. This is particularly true if the dinghy to be towed is waterlogged, or if it is much larger than the towing vessel.

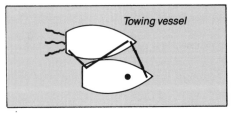

Towing alongside

To set up a tow alongside, three lines are usually needed: a bow rope, a stern rope and a back spring led from the bow of the towing vessel to the stern of the casualty. Make sure that the towed vessel's stern is well ahead of the stern of the towboat, or manoeuvring will be very difficult.

When towing in line, the last dinghy should be the only one with the rudder in position. This method is not completely satisfactory because all the strain is taken on the first boat.

The alternative is the Herringbone tow, with boats secured at intervals on either

side of a main towline. Sailing clubs and centres which often use this method usually have a floating towline with loops at intervals along its length. Boats wishing to take a tow simply secure to the loop with

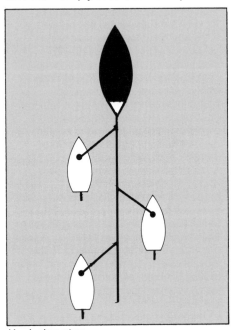

Herringbone tow

their own painters, using a round turn and two half-hitches. If there are no loops, the rolling hitch is the correct one to secure a painter to the towline.

The important practical differences between this and a tow in line are that all the boats must be steered and that the painters are best led straight from the mast – not through a bow fairlead. When splitting a herringbone tow, the towing vessel may hold station head to wind. This allows each dinghy crew to hoist their sails and leave the tow at will. If the spacing between adjacent dinghies is not generous, it may be safer for the last boat in the tow to cast off first, and so on.

Man overboard recovery

Although MOB recovery is included in the Level 2 course, it is repeated at Level 3 to ensure that you have the opportunity to master this important technique. The basic principles are:

"So what's in it for me?"

RYA

RYA
MEMBERSHIP
FORM

ROYAL YACHTING ASSOCIATION

ROYAL YACHTING ASSOCIATION

"We can hel arrange documentatio

Imagine a boating world where legislation took away all your freedom to enjoy the water in the way you always have – the way you enjoy.

Imagine a time when Brussels dictated to the UK the documents each yacht should carry.

Suppose there were no official judges and umpires to adjudicate races, no Olympic team to represent this country at the Games.

Imagine having no-one to fight our case for the fair use of coastal and inland waters

Imagine a boating world without the RYA.
Just £17 will help protect your boating future.

> **ou to buy your boat safely, ining courses, provide offer help and advice...**

By joining the RYA you gain access to a large group of experts and professionals who can provide boating and legal advice for all aspects of your sport.

You can benefit from this expertise by joining now... and by simply picking up the phone next time you need advice.

You also get...

- *FREE* 'RYA News', the quarterly magazine of the RYA
- *FREE* Allocation of T, Y and M sail numbers
- *FREE* International Certificates of Competence (if you qualify)
- *FREE* RYA voucher for books worth £5 – possibly much more
- *FREE* Third party insurance cover for windsurfers
- RYA Visa Card* No annual fee (subject to status)

Special Discounts on...

- *Insurance.* 10% (more with qualifications) discount on most yacht and dinghy policies through RYA Brokers, Bishop Skinner.
- *Hospital and Medical Care Association.* Up to 40% discount.
- *Car Rental.* 20% discount through Europcar Interrent.
- *Class Certificates.* Special reductions on RYA administered racing classes.

Membership costs...

£19 for an adult (£17 for direct debit).
£8 for a youth (under 21).

R Y A M E M B E R S H I P

Please use block capitals

NAME
Mr/Mrs/Miss _____

Address _____

_____

_____

_____ Postcode _____

Type of Membership Required (tick as applicable)

☐ **Personal** £19.00 (£17.00 if you pay by Direct Debit)

☐ **Under 21** £8.00

Under 21 Date of Birth [   ]

Signed [   ]

My principal boating interest is: (tick 1 box only)

Windsurfing ☐   Sail Cruising ☐   Motor Cruising ☐   Sail Racing ☐   Powerboat Racing ☐

THE EASY WAY TO PAY Originators identification number: 955213
INSTRUCTIONS TO YOUR BANK OR BUILDING SOCIETY TO PAY DIRECT DEBITS

◖ DIRECT Debit

Please complete parts 1 to 5 to instruct your bank or building society to make payments directly from your account.
Then return the form to **Royal Yachting Association, RYA House, Romsey Road, Eastleigh, Hants. SO50 9YA. Tel: 01703 629962, Fax: 01703 629924.**

1. Name of Account Holder [   ]

2. Account number [ ][ ][ ][ ][ ][ ][ ][ ]

3. Sort Code [ ][ ][ ] — [ ][ ] — [ ][ ]

4. Please write the full postal address of your bank or building society branch in the box below

To: The Manager _____

_____

_____

_____

_____ Postcode _____

Banks or Building Society may refuse to accept instructions to pay Direct Debits from some types of account.

5. Your instructions to the bank or building society and signature.
• I instruct you to pay Direct Debits from my account at the request of the Royal Yachting Association.
• The amounts are variable and are to be debited on various dates.
• I understand that the Royal Yachting Association may change the amounts and dates only after giving me prior notice.
• I will inform the bank or building society in writing if I wish to cancel these instructions.
• I understand that if any Direct Debit is paid which breaks the terms of the instruction, the bank or building society will make a refund.
Signature(s):

[   ]

Date: [   ]

RYA MEMBERSHIP FORM

Cash, Cheque, Postal Order
enclosed £ [   ] Made payable to the Royal Yachting Association

077   **Office use only:** Membership No. Allocated [   ]

Office use/ Centre Stamp

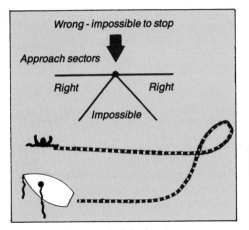

Wrong - impossible to stop

Approach sectors

Right   *Right*

Impossible

★ regain control of the boat
★ sail off on a beam reach, letting the jib fly
★ try to keep an eye on the man in the water, who will have inflated his lifejacket and should hold up a hand and shout to keep in touch
★ when you are a suitable distance away, tack onto a reciprocal course. That distance will vary according to weather conditions, but the principle is that it is just far enough to give you room for the rest of the manoeuvre
★ as you get closer, sail slightly downwind so that your final approach can be on a close reach, allowing you to control your speed
★ stop with the man at your weather shroud
★ as you move forward to help him, flick the tiller to windward and position yourself just behind the weather shroud. That flick stops the boat inadvertently tacking on top of the man while you are struggling to retrieve him.

The only difficult part of the manoeuvre during a course is the judgement of boat speed on your final approach. Practise it often. If it happens for real, the most difficult part could be getting the man back aboard; try rocking the boat to dip the gunwhale. Don't try hauling him in over the transom. The boat will bear away and begin to sail off out of control; the tiller is easily damaged and, worse still, it is not pleasant to be dragged over a sharp-edged, gadget-littered transom. As a last resort, you might have to capsize deliberately to scoop the man back aboard.

Finally, if it happens for real you might have to right the dinghy anyway, since the sudden loss of crew weight may well have caused a capsize. At least in this case you probably won't have the MOB recovery to worry about, for unless the man is injured he should be able to swim to the capsized dinghy.

Sailing to best advantage

This part of the RYA Level 5 Advanced Skills course aims to polish the techniques learnt earlier. Perhaps the most important aspects of pure sailing are summarised in the 'Five Essentials' – sail setting, boat balance, fore and aft trim, centreboard position and course made good.

Sail setting

You know that each sail, whether mainsail, jib or spinnaker will set best when eased until it just starts to flap along the luff and then pulled in just enough to stop the flapping. At this point there is an even flow of air across both sides of the sail.

As an aid to sail trim, the flow can easily be monitored by the use of telltales; lengths of wool or nylon strips sewn into jib or mainsail luffs and onto mainsail leeches. At the first level of their use, telltales give a clear indication of whether the airflow at that point on the sail is smooth or stalled. They are most commonly seen on jib luffs and used as shown in the diagram.

At another level of use, such jib luff telltales will indicate whether the sheeting angle is correct. If it is, all of the telltales will respond to a change in unison. If the sheeting angle is too far aft, the top telltale will lift before the others and conversely if the sheeting angle is too far forward, the bottom telltale will lift first.

Similarly, mainsail leech telltales indicate whether the sail is oversheeted and if sail twist is right for the conditions, such that all the telltales stream together. If the leech is too twisted the top telltale will stall first and vice versa. Kicker, mainsheet and traveller adjustments provide the cure.

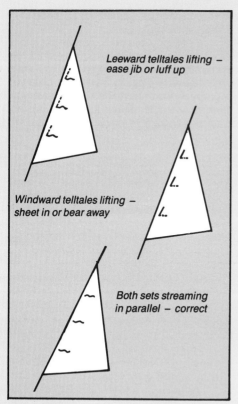

Leeward telltales lifting –
ease jib or luff up

Windward telltales lifting –
sheet in or bear away

Both sets streaming
in parallel – correct

Using telltales

Boat balance

You know that dinghies sail fastest when upright, but at this level you should be thinking a little beyond that simple truth. The exception to the rule is in very light winds, when some heel may help by reducing the wetted hull surface which

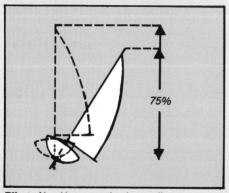

75%

Effect of heel in presenting less sail area

causes the greater drag component at low speeds. It also helps by causing the sail to take up its designed shape due to gravity, thus creating an efficient aerofoil for what little wind there is.

The effects of heel are not new to you; nor is the fact that a heeled rig presents less effective sail area. What may be new is the concept of using the effects to make your manoeuvres smoother. In particular, by heeling the boat to windward in stronger winds you will make the process of bearing away look simple. Contrast that to the struggle seen when someone tries to bear away in a boat which is already heeled to leeward. Active use of body weight is the key.

Fore and aft trim

Once again, we need to progress from the basic advice about keeping the boat flat to consider active use of body weight.

Sailing to windward, crew weight should be concentrated forward in all conditions. In light weather, it serves to reduce wetted surface area and hence drag, whilst in stronger winds it promotes bow immersion and hence prevents the bow being knocked off to leeward by waves, which increases leeway.

Offwind, crew weight is moved progressively aft depending on hull shape, wind direction and strength. The stronger and freer the wind, the further aft you sit. Most dinghy hulls are designed with flat aft sections for planing in moderate or strong winds; to promote planing you need to get the bow sections clear of the water. That also helps the steering characteristics and counters the pitching moment of the rig which is trying to make you nosedive.

Whether sailing upwind or down, the crew should work as a team, concentrating body weight together. This reduces windage and the pitching caused by wave action.

Centreboard position

All that needs to be said at this level is at every alteration of course should be matched by an almost instinctive change in centreboard position. In stronger winds it is sometime preferable to raise the centreboard a little even when beating in order to reduce heeling; the theory is that leeway is reduced anyway due to the higher boat speed.

Course made good

Plan your route to take the greatest advantage of favourable factors and the least ill effects of contrary factors. On any water you are subject to windshifts, and your course made good will take advantage of freeing shifts and steer you away from headers.

Sailing offwind on inland waters, free of obstructions to water or wind, your best course made good will probably be a straight line between departure and destination. In planing conditions, this route will of course be modified by the alterations needed to take best advantage of gusts.

At all other times, you'll have to weigh

At sea, you'll have the extra dimension of the tide. The basic principle of staying in a fair tide and out of a foul one is clear enough, but at this level you should be thinking about rather more than that. Tides flow faster in channels and around headlands, so plan your route accordingly. Assuming you can tack efficiently, it will pay you to short-tack along the shore in shallow water rather than take long hitches out into the tide.

Spinnaker handling

The correct use of a spinnaker adds greatly to the efficiency and enjoyment of dinghy sailing. Whilst it is not a difficult sail to master, the early stages of spinnaker handling practice do take up a great deal of searoom and you will find it easier to practise the hoisting, lowering and gybing drills ashore in light weather before going afloat.

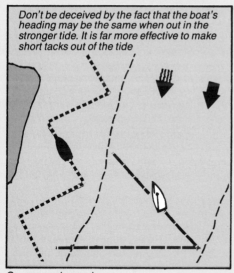

Don't be deceived by the fact that the boat's heading may be the same when out in the stronger tide. It is far more effective to make short tacks out of the tide

Course made good

up the relative benefits of different routes. When sailing on still waters inland, the wind shadows caused by buildings or trees might be your only concern. On rivers, the current probably causes the greatest consideration – stay out in the middle when sailing with it, keep to the edges when against the flow. Find out how the current flows around bends in the river (usually faster on the outside).

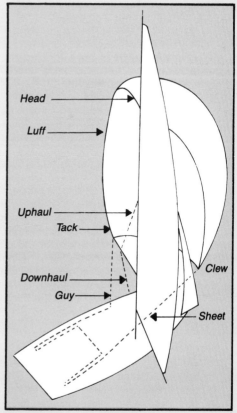

Head
Luff
Uphaul
Tack
Clew
Downhaul
Guy
Sheet

The spinnaker – essential terms

Before going into the detailed drills for handling the sail, it is worth making a few points about spinnaker setting. The sail is only used with the wind abaft the beam and always set with the pole on the windward side of the boat.

As a rough guide to setting the spinnaker pole, you should aim to keep it at 90 degrees to the apparent wind, with the pole height adjusted so that the two clews of the sail are at the same height.

The spinnaker is then sheeted in just the same way as any other sail, easing the sheet until the luff just curls and then sheeting in until there is no curl. Constant attention is needed to get maximum drive, although the guy will be adjusted far less often than the sheet.

Hoisting and lowering the spinnaker

There are two popular systems for stowing the spinnaker, either a spinnaker chute or a system of spinnaker bags. On some dinghies there is neither, the crew having to rely on the sail being stowed in a bucket! The spinnaker chute is somewhat easier to use than bags, but it adds weight to the bow of the dinghy and causes more wear on the spinnaker than the other methods.

The hoisting and lowering drills given below apply to boats using spinnaker bags. If using a chute, simply follow the leeward hoist and drop drills.

If your dinghy has two bags, you should learn all the methods for hoists and drops although the leeward drop is far less often used than the windward drop, because of the resulting instability. The final alternative may be used when the spinnaker is simply packed in a bucket and the halyard and sheets all have quick-release clips. It is then possible to opt always for leeward hoist and windward drop (the easiest choices) provided you remember to move the sheets and halyard accordingly.

Leeward spinnaker hoist

The spinnaker is stowed to leeward and the halyard is led aft to the helmsman. The important principle about this hoist is that the pole must be set before the spinnaker is hoisted.

★ Helmsman prepares to pass the spinnaker pole to the crew. Crew clears the spinnaker for hoisting
★ Helmsman passes pole to crew and balances the boat
★ Crew clips pole to guy, fits uphaul/downhaul and clips pole to mast
★ Helmsman hoists spinnaker and cleats halyard. Frees sheet. Crew adjusts and cleats guy
★ Helmsman adjusts sheet if crew is still adjusting guy. Crew then takes over sheet and plays it
★ Helmsman sits to leeward if necessary so that crew can sit to windward, where he will have a clear view of the spinnaker luff and wind indicators.

Windward spinnaker hoist

The spinnaker is stowed to windward and the halyard led aft to the helmsman. The important difference in principle between this and the leeward hoist is that the spinnaker is hoisted and thrown forward before the pole is attached.

★ Helmsman prepares to pass pole to crew, who frees sheets and halyard
★ Helmsman places pole ready for crew to pick up easily. Crew sets guy and cleats it so that the windward clew can reach the forestay
★ Helmsman takes up slack in halyard. Crew picks up spinnaker in as tight a bundle as possible, whilst holding the sheet in the other hand
★ Helmsman steers downwind and hoists the spinnaker when the crew hails. He will bear away onto a run if necessary. Crew calls to helmsman to hoist. Crew throws the spinnaker forward, pulling on sheet until spinnaker is clear to leeward
★ Helmsman comes back on course. Crew fits pole and adjusts and cleats guy
★ Helmsman sets spinnaker sheet. Crew takes sheet from helmsman
★ If necessary, helmsman sits to leeward so that crew can sit to windward.

Windward spinnaker drop

Apart from on boats with chutes, when a variation of the leeward drop is used, this technique is to be favoured.

★ Crew eases guy forward, removes pole and passes it to helmsman
★ Helmsman takes and stows pole. Crew releases sheet
★ Crew stands by windward side of mast, takes guy and gathers foot of spinnaker until leeward clew passes round forestay
★ Helmsman releases halyard on instruction of crew. Crew stows spinnaker by first working down windward luff
★ Both tidy and cleat halyard and sheets.

Leeward spinnaker drop

Remember that in strong winds this method is not advised, as it requires the crew to be on the leeward side of the boat.

★ Crew eases guy forward and pulls in on sheet
★ Helmsman lowers halyard
★ Crew pulls rapidly on clew working down leech of spinnaker and stows it in bag
★ Crew removes pole. Helmsman balances boat
★ Crew tidies and cleats halyard and sheets.

Gybing the spinnaker

The aim should be to keep the spinnaker full throughout the gybe. The basic principle is that the mainsail is gybed first and then the helmsman sails the boat under the spinnaker whilst the crew attends to the pole.

★ Helmsman squares off onto a dead run. Crew centres spinnaker and cleats sheet and guy
★ Helmsman gybes mainsail slowly, pausing amidships. Crew gybes jib, unclips pole from mast and clips to old sheet
Helmsman plays new sheet to keep spinnaker full. Crew unclips pole from old guy and clips to mast

★ Helmsman luffs onto new course. Crew trims guy and sheet as required.

Trapeze work

The function of the trapeze is simply to enable the crew to exert more of a righting moment on the boat by getting his body weight further out. With a few notable exceptions including some multihulls, trapeze boats tend also to be equipped with spinnakers – the two go together.

There are two simple rules for wearing trapeze harnesses – position the hook near your body's centre of gravity (i.e. near the navel) and secure the harness as tightly as you comfortably can.

When trapezing, the first important principle is that the pull on the trapeze wire will tend always to pull you forward and this must be resisted by bracing your forward foot.

To go out on the wire, first hook on and ensure that your weight is taken on the hook, rather than on the handle. When going out, always lead with your front foot. Swing out over the gunwhale and push yourself out with the front foot until you are in the right position.

When coming back in, bend both knees and then take the back foot off the gunwhale first to swing back inboard.

Except in marginal conditions, always try to keep your body flat when trapezing. You'll find that the trapeze gear includes either a double hook or a tackle which allows you to adjust the height of the hook.

If it's the former, the principle is that you use the long hook to keep your weight really low down for beating, whilst the short hook will keep you slightly higher and make it easier for you to come in and out more often when reaching. The tackle gives you the ability to adjust the hook height at will, even when you are out on it.

In marginal conditions, it is far better for the helmsman to adjust his weight frequently to allow the crew to stay out longer on the wire; teamwork is important for smooth trapezing.

Sailing a circular course

This exercise is very popular with Instructors and Coaches as it provides a very compact way of practising or assessing boat handling. You should aim to complete a neat circle repetitively around a stationary, free floating object such as a dory, the radius of the circle being no more than three boat lengths.

With practice, you should be able to bring the radius down to one boat length, still meeting the criterion that, should the action be "frozen" at any moment, everything is perfectly suited to the point of sailing. The exception to this will be that, as the circle becomes smaller, so the crew will have to leave the centreboard in one position.

Each tack and gybe should be smooth and the boat should remain upright throughout. The beauty of this exercise is that, if you have the ability, you can keep up the circling almost indefinitely whereas if you are not totally in control of your tacking and gybing, you will end up in a tangle of tiller extension and mainsheet.

Boat handling in adverse circumstances

Sailing without a centreboard

Accepting that a centreboard is vital to the dinghy's efficiency, the aim of sailing without one is to minimise the loss of pointing ability.

To a certain extent, hard chine dinghies respond to being heeled to leeward so that a chine is immersed for extra grip on the water, but this technique is obviously useless on round-bilge boats. Try moving crew weight well forward to immerse the vee-sections of the bow.

To make windward progress, accept that you're not going to point high so sail fast and free to minimise leeway. Try to establish just how much leeway you're making and plan your route accordingly. Make the most of windshifts and any tidal differences but above all make extra allowance for obstructions; if in doubt sail to leeward or downtide of any hazards.

Sailing without a rudder

Once the basic techniques are mastered, this can be one of the dinghy sailor's most satisfying skills. In the early stages, prepare the boat and choose your weather well.

The basic principle of sailing rudderless is to use the effects of sails and boat balance to steer. You'll find it much easier to do if you reduce the number of variables to a minimum.

★ Tell your crew to sit motionless on the boat's centreline, only moving if you decided. Keep all crew weight well forward

★ Knot the jibsheets together to make them easier to handle and if you are sailing in light winds, reduce the number of purchases in the mainsheet for more positive control

★ Raise the centreboard by a third to move the centre of lateral resistance aft. This will reduce the sensitivity of the boat to your movements

Sail to a clear stretch of water then, with mainsheet in one hand and jibsheets in the other, you're ready to start. Begin on a reach and find out how changes in sail trim affect the course sailed.

Every type of boat responds differently, but you'll find that the mainsail has far more effect in causing the dinghy to luff than the jib has in helping to bear away, hence the centreboard position.

You will also find that sheeting in the mainsail alone will be enough to make you tack, but that bearing away will require the combined effect of the jib and windward heel. With practice, you will be able to handle the dinghy on any point of sailing.

To a distant observer, it should appear that the rudder is still in place, so positive is the boat handling. You should have no difficulty in either sailing to windward, tacking or gybing.

SAILING THEORY AND BACKGROUND

Sea terms

The boat

Fore and aft	– In line from bow to stern; on or parallel to the centreline
Amidships	– In the middle of the boat
Bow	– The forward part of the boat
Stern	– The aftermost part of the boat
Quarter	– The part on each side behind 'amidships', i.e. the rear corners
Port	– Left hand side facing forwards
Starboard	– Right hand side facing forwards

Position relative to the boat

Windward	– The side from which the wind is blowing
Leeward	– The side away from the wind direction (pronounced loo'ard)
Abeam	– At right angles to the centreline
Ahead	– In front of the boat
Astern	– Behind the boat
To weather	– To windward
Forward	– Near or towards the bow
Aft	– Near or towards the stern
Downwind	– To leeward.

Boat manoeuvres

Tacking	– Loosely used to mean the same as 'going'about' – turning the bow of the boat through the wind. In racing terms, a dinghy is tacking strictly from the moment when the wind is dead ahead until she has borne away on the new course
Gybing	– Turning the stern through the wind. Strictly, a dinghy is gybing when, with the wind aft, the foot of her mainsail crosses her centreline. She completes the gybe when the mainsail has filled on the new tack

In irons	– Stationary head to wind
By the lee	– Running with the wind on same side as boom
Planing	– Sailing fast enough to rise up over own bow wave and reach speeds not related to waterline length
To luff	– Turning towards the wind without tacking
To bear away	– Turning further away from the wind
To pinch	– Trying to sail closer to the wind than close hauled, with the effect that the sails flap
Sternway	– A dinghy is making sternway when moving backwards under control
Broaching	– Uncontrolled movement towards the wind.

International Regulations for Preventing Collisions at Sea

By the time you reach Level 3 of the National Dinghy Certificate, you should already know the basic rules about sailing vessels meeting, but the diagrams will act as a reminder.

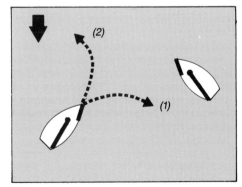

Port and starboard
If you are on port tack, either turn behind the other boat (1) or tack (2)

If you are on starboard tack, keep going. If at the last minute you think the other person hasn't seen you, tack

23

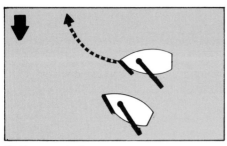

On the same tack
Windward boat gives way

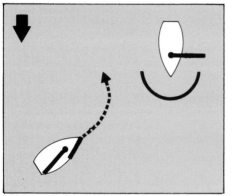

When in doubt about the other boat
If port tack boat cannot decide which tack the
windward boat is on, she must give way

Meeting power driven vessels

The basic principle is that the power driven vessel shall keep out of the way of the sailing vessel, but there are important exceptions to that principle.

A sailing vessel shall not impede the passage of a power driven vessel which is navigating within a narrow channel or traffic lane. In practical terms, the only times you are likely to come across ships when you are dinghy sailing is when they are in what are narrow channels to them, even though they may be wide open spaces to you.

In addition, sailing vessels shall keep out of the way of fishing vessels and other vessels restricted in their ability to manoeuvre.

In narrow channels

If you are following a channel, keep to the starboard side. If you have to beat up a channel, remember the rule about not impeding much larger vessels.

If you are crossing a narrow channel, you must do so as nearly as possible at right angles, again making sure you do not impede the passage of vessels following the channel.

Action by stand-on vessel

The International Regulations lay down a clear set of responsibilities afloat, which include the action of both vessels in any potential collision. If the other vessel is required to keep out of your way, then you shall keep your course and speed.

That gives the other vessel the opportunity to take suitable action without the possibility of confusion. As soon as it becomes clear to you that the other vessel is not taking appropriate action, you may alter course or speed to avoid her.

Even if you are the stand-on vessel and you find yourself so close that collision cannot be avoided by the action of the other vessel alone, then you must take suitable avoiding action.

Weather information

Anyone taking a boat to sea should have some insight into what the weather is going to do. It is unwise for the dinghy sailor to rely totally on the Shipping Forecasts prepared by the Met Office and broadcast by the BBC.

These forecasts cover huge areas and are thus bound to be general, rather than specific. The dinghy sailor should supplement this broad picture with more detailed local information. For current times of all forecast sources outlined below, consult the National Press.

Forecasts on BBC radio

Shipping Forecasts on Radio 4 (200 kHz and 1500m) are the main source of weather information for the sea areas between South Iceland and Cape Finisterre. They are broadcast about every six hours and include gale warnings in operation, a general synopsis, forecasts for the different sea areas and reports of actual weather from selected stations.

A little practice and some form of shorthand are needed to write down all the relevant information in the time available. Weather forecast maps and forms are useful aids. Shipping forecasts provide good background information for the dinghy sailor, but the information is often not very specific.

Inshore Waters Forecasts on Radio 3 (medium wave and VHF) are broadcast less frequently, but serve to build up the general picture of coastal conditions. Once again, the forecasts cover huge areas at a time.

Land area forecasts do not give any detailed information on wind strength or direction but give a useful indication of general weather trends.

Local radio stations

Most local radio stations provide weather forecasts which are most useful for dinghy sailors since they are local. Many of the stations located in popular sailing areas have special forecasts for sailors and windsurfers.

TV Forecasts

Met satellite pictures and computer graphics have made TV forecasts one of the clearest forms of general weather information. They cannot give local detail but provide an invaluable picture of the overall weather pattern.

Telephone Forecasts

Marinecall offers dedicated recorded message forecasts for yachtsmen at premium rates, with a complete regional framework of service.

Press

Newspaper forecasts are inevitably out of date, when compared with many of the other sources of information. Whilst they give a general background to the weather pattern they should not be relied on by dinghy sailors as a sole source.

Coastguards and Harbour Masters

The local Coastguard station (if appropriate) and the Harbour Master's office are useful sources of information and often have local updates from other nearby sources.

Gale warnings

These are broadcast if a gale is expected somewhere in the sea area and do not necessarily apply to the whole of that area. Of more use to the dinghy sailor are the Strong Wind Warnings broadcast on local radio when winds at Force 6 or above are expected.

Main characteristics of high and low pressure areas

Gradient wind is caused by a movement of air from regions of high pressure to regions of low pressure. Britain's weather pattern tends to be very changeable as we are largely influenced by areas of low pressure coming in from the Atlantic, bringing with them strong winds.

In the summer, this pattern is interrupted by the appearance of anticyclones or large areas of high pressure, which bring warmer settled weather and lighter winds.

Depressions are areas of low pressure with air circulating in an anti-clockwise direction rather like a whirlpool. On weather maps they appear as swirls of isobars (the lines joining places of equal pressure). The closer the isobars to each other, the stronger the wind. Low pressure systems tend to bring with them wind, cloud and rain.

High pressure systems or anticyclones bring with them light, variable winds and warm weather. The air moves clockwise around the system and in an outwards direction. High pressure systems have no definite path of travel and may linger for several days at a time before being pushed out of the way by depressions.

Major changes in pressure

We have already seen that anticyclones are large areas with little change in pressure which result in good, settled weather. We have also seen that the closer the isobars on a synoptic chart, the stronger the wind. These are just two practical examples of the relationship between changes in barometric pressure and wind strength.

The principal reason for keeping a barograph at a sailing club or centre is so that a clear indication of the rate of change of barometric pressure may be available. Rapidly falling or rapidly rising pressure provides a sure guide to a change in weather conditions brought by the strong winds.

Local Conditions

In good weather conditions, especially during the summer months, much of the coastline experiences sea breezes. The heat of the sun warms up the land, which causes the air above it to warm up and rise. Cooler air from above the sea is drawn in to replace it.

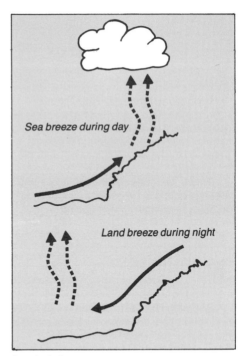

Sea breeze during day

Land breeze during night

Local winds

This sea breeze usually starts during the late morning and reaches its peak in mid-afternoon. One of the tell-tale signs of a sea breeze is the line of cloud along the coastline in an otherwise clear summer sky.

If there is already an onshore wind blowing, its strength will be increased by the sea breeze whereas if the gradient wind is offshore, the effect of the sea breeze will be to reduce or even cancel it.

On days which have seen sea breezes the opposite effect is felt during the evening. The land and the air cool much faster than the sea and so the land breeze becomes established.

Beaufort wind scale

Designed as a means of grouping associated sets of wind strengths and sea states, the Beaufort scale serves as a form of code or "shorthand" for all who go to sea. Thus if a forecast indicates a Force 4, you can have a good idea not only of the wind speed to expect, but also the sea state which will be generated in open water. You will also have an idea of what sort of sailing you can expect, according to your ability.

Beaufort Force	General description	Sea Criterion	Land Criterion	Windspeed in knots
0	Calm	Sea like a mirror	Calm; smoke rises vertically	below 1
1	Light air	Ripples with appearance of scales are formed but without foam crests	Wind direction shown by smoke drift but not by wind vanes	1 to 3
2	Light breeze	Small wavelets, still short but more pronounced. Crests have a glassy appearance and do not break	Wind felt on face; leaves rustle; ordinary vane moved by wind	4 to 6
3	Gentle breeze	Large wavelets. Crests begin to break. Foam of glassy appearance. Perhaps scattered white horses	Leaves and small twigs in constant motion. Wind extends light flags	7 to 10
4	Moderate breeze	Small waves becoming longer; fairly frequent white horses	Raises dust and loose paper; small branches are moved	11 to 16
5	Fresh breeze	Moderate waves, taking more pronounced long form; many white horses are formed. Chance of some spray	Small trees in leaf begin to sway. Crested wavelets form on inland waters	17 to 21
6	Strong breeze	Large waves begin to form; white foam crests are more extensive everywhere. Probably some spray	Large branches in motion; whistling heard in telephone wires, umbrellas used with difficulty	22 to 27
7	Near gale	Sea heaps up and white foam from breaking waves begin to be blown in streaks along the direction of the wind	Whole trees in motion; inconvenience felt when walking against wind	28 to 33
8	Gale	Moderately high waves of greater length; edges of crests begin to break into spin-drift. The foam is blown in well-marked streaks along the direction of the wind	Breaks twigs off trees; generally impedes progress	34 to 40
9	Severe gale	High waves. Dense streaks of foam along the direction of the wind. Crests of waves begin to topple, tumble and roll over. Spray may affect visibility	Slight structural damage occurs (chimney pots and slates removed)	41 to 47
10	Storm	Very high waves with long overhanging crest. Resulting foam in great patches is blown in dense streaks along the direction of the wind. Whole surface takes on a white appearance. Tumbling of sea becomes heavy and shock-like. Visibility affected	Seldom experienced inland; trees uprooted; considerable structural damage occurs	48 to 55

The most important difference between inland and coastal sailing is the tide, which can affect almost every part of your sailing. It can dictate where and when you get afloat, where you can go and how long it will take you to get there. When related to wind direction, it can even dictate how rough or uncomfortable the passage will be.

Tides are caused by the gravitational attraction of the Earth, Moon and Sun, together with the rotation of the Earth. The Sun has only about a third of the influence of the Moon on the tides. When Moon and Sun pull together, the very high and low tides called Spring tides are produced. When they work against each other, the smaller neap tides result.

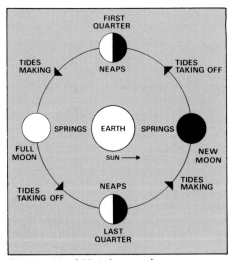

Relationship of tide to lunar cycle

Times and heights of high and low water are found in Admiralty Tide Tables and nautical almanacs, but both of these publications are far more comprehensive than the typical dinghy sailor requires. Local tide tables available from yacht chandlers, sailing clubs or the Harbourmaster provide the simple information required for any single place.

Because the water level is constantly changing due to the tide, a standard reference point is needed for charts. The point taken for a chart datum approximates to the lowest expected level of the tide, known as the Lowest Astronomical Tide or LAT.

As you can see from the diagram, the heights of high and low water and most of the other points are referred to this datum. The difference in height between each high water and the next low water (or vice versa) is known as the range of that tide.

Rule of twelfths

If you have proper tide tables or an almanac, there is a simple graphical way of working out intermediate tidal heights and times. If not, the rule of twelfths provides a rough guide.

Based on the assumption that the tide follows a symmetrical flow pattern during a 12 hour cycle between successive high waters, the rule nevertheless provides enough accuracy for most dinghy sailing.

During the 1st hour after HW, the range is 1/12 of the total;

During the 2nd hour after HW, the range is 2/12 of the total;

During the 3rd hour after HW, the range is 3/12 of the total;

During the 4th hour after HW, the range is 3/12 of the total;

During the 5th hour after HW, the range is 2/12 of the total;

During the 6th hour after HW, the range is 1/12 of the total.

To use the rule, you only need to know the time and height of either high or low water, together with the range for that tide.

Example

HW time is 1400; HW height is 8m
Range is 6m
What is height of tide at 1800?
Range divided by 12 = ½m
1800 is 4 hours after HW i.e. 9/12 of the range
9/12 of 6m is 4.5m i.e. tide will have fallen by 4.5m
8m − 4.5m = 3.5m
Height of tide at 1800 is 3.5m

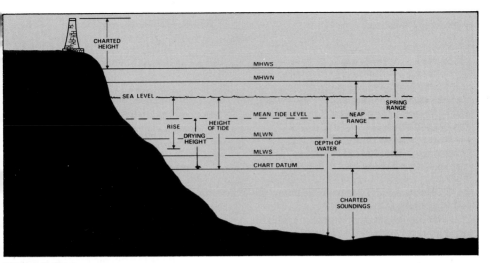

Tidal definitions

Finally, to get the depth of water in any spot at a certain time, you need only add the charted depth to that figure for height of tide. Thus in the previous example, if the question had asked for the depth of water at 1800 in a spot whose charted depth was 3m, the answer would have been 6.5m.

To find the rates of tidal streams, either consult the chart or use special tidal stream atlases, which include diagrams showing the tidal streams for a given area, all related to times before or after High Water at the nearest appropriate port.

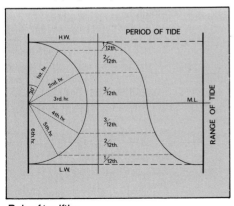

Rule of twelfths

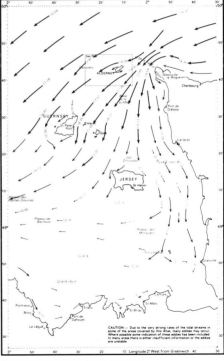

Extract from Tidal Stream Atlas

29

The compass

Whether cruising or racing a dinghy, a compass is a very useful item of equipment. The steering compass is graduated from 0 to 360 degrees, the circular card being mounted on a fine point and suspended in a bowl of fluid to dampen the oscillations.

The compass needle will indicate magnetic north, although the chart is aligned to true north. The difference between them is known as Variation and varies with time and with your location, but it is indicated on the chart.

The majority of steering compasses have a mark on the rim called the 'lubber line' to indicate the boat's head and hence help you steer a given course.

Nobody can steer a small craft absolutely accurately but the competent helmsman should be able to keep to within 5 degrees of the required course, with errors in one direction being compensated by errors the other way.

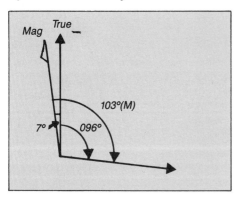

Compass variation. In this example, with variation of 7° West, a true bearing of 096° equals a magnetic bearing of 103°

The compass is subject to disturbance called Deviation from ferrous metal objects nearby. These are likely to be few in a dinghy but it is worth checking the effect of any metal fittings when you are installing a compass by putting it near them and seeing whether the card swings. In a cruising dinghy, don't forget to stow things like an outboard engine and even beercans well away from the compass.

Interpretation of charts

Charts are a representation of a curved surface of the earth on a flat sheet of paper. As a result, charts are drawn using a system of latitude and longitude as a grid reference and a scale. Distance is always measured on the latitude scale (up the side of the chart) where one minute of latitude is equal to one nautical mile. The vertical lines on the chart all relate to true north.

Charts vary in scale according to their purpose. For the dinghy sailor the large scale chart covering a relatively small area but in great detail is the most useful.

Every chart is full of information, most of it given by means of a wide range of symbols. They are all listed in Chart 5011 (which is actually a booklet). To keep charts updated with changes in lights, buoys or other importnt features, use the weekly Notices to Mariners or quarterly Small Craft Edition published by the Admiralty.

Buoyage

The IALA system of buoyage is used throughout Europe and applies to all fixed and floating marks. The system covers both lateral buoyage (marking the sides of navigable channels) and cardinal buoyage (used to indicate the position of hazards or navigational features relative to compass direction). Your knowledge of buoyage must be used in conjunction with a chart, to indicate the position of the buoys and the nature of the hazards, if any, which they mark.

A useful principle to remember when cruising in a dinghy is that the buoyage system is in use principally for the masters of larger vessels. Assuming that you have enough water, you might actually be safer sailing outside the limits of navigable channels as you would be safe from shipping.

Full details of the IALA system of buoyage are given in a poster produce by the RYA Seamanship Foundation, in the Seaway Code and in the majority of sailing books, so they do not need to be repeated here.

Transits

Although buoys form the principal aid to pilotage, the dinghy sailor will often find it valuable to be able to use transits. A transit is formed when two identifiable objects are brought in line with each other.

If those objects are in line, you know you must be on a position line extending through the objects. This gives a very accurate position line without reference to the compass or any other navigational aid.

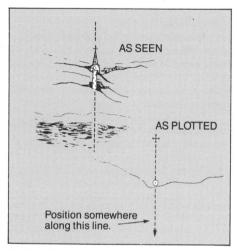

Position line by transit

In some cases, transits are deliberately established, such as leading marks or lights set up to guide you in to a harbour entrance. In other cases the transits can be less formal ones. You might see from local sailing directions that the transit formed by keeping one headland clear of another will keep you out of the danger line of rocks or a shoal.

When using transits, it is wise to check with a compass bearing to ensure that you have identified the objects correctly.

Position fixing by bearings

The hand bearing compass allows you to measure the magnetic bearing from other objects to your position. If you take the bearing of a known object using a hand bearing compass and then relate that to the chart, you must be on a given position line from that object.

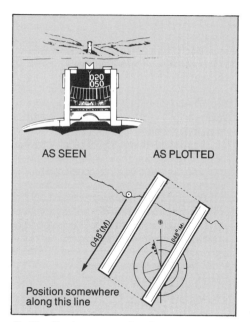

Position line by compass bearing

By taking the bearings of two objects, you can establish your position with certainty as the point where the position lines meet. For the smallest error, choose objects as nearly as possible at right angles to each other.

Ideally, a third object will confirm your fix exactly, but in practice you will find that a fix from three objects will give a 'cocked hat' area of uncertainty. Assume you are in the centre of that area unless you need to play safe by assuming that you are closest to your nearest point of danger.

Practical pilotage in a dinghy is difficult. You might prefer to work in Magnetic bearings all the time, to avoid possible errors in converting to True. You will also find that a plotting instrument like a Breton Plotter will be much easier to use than the parallel rules of formal navigation.

Even a plotter may be difficult to use at times, so part of your planning might include drawing radial lines from known objects at, say, 10 degree intervals in order to make life easier when afloat. Equally, a few notes written on the chart before you slip it into its protective covering might help you remember important details.

Dead reckoning and estimated position

Dinghy cruising in coastal waters in good visibility usually requires no more than pilotage. There are times, however, when the cruising dinghy sailor will need to know how to establish position by dead reckoning – that is reckoning deduced from log and compass.

In practical terms this can be no more than an approximation, because very few cruising dinghies carry a log for measuring speed or distance run through the water.

The principle, however, is that if you know the direction and distance you have sailed from a given start position, you can quickly establish where you are.

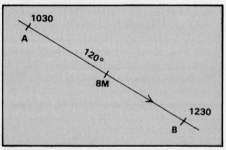

Principle of dead reckoning – if a dinghy starts from A at 1030 and sails for two hours at 4 knots on a course of 120°(M), then at 1230 her DR position is B

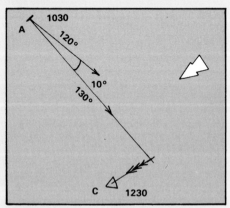

Estimated position – although the course steered and distance run are the same as the previous example, 10° leeway and a tidal stream setting 230° at one knot have been added to give an estimated position C at 1230

To convert this simple dead reckoning into something more useful, it is necessary to add two corrections – leeway and tidal streams. Leeway must be estimated by comparing the dinghy's wake with her course. In practice, leeway will be negigible when reaching or running but could be as much as 10 degrees when beating.

The direction and rate of the tidal stream comes, as outlined earlier, from the chart or tidal stream atlas. Once leeway and tide have been taken into account, the position by dead reckoning can be converted to an estimated position, as shown.

Establishing a course to steer

The basic principles outlined above show how to find your position by dead reckoning; in other words working from history. The opposite task for the navigator is to establish a course to steer to allow for tide and leeway.

This will not apply when beating, as you will try to sail as close to the wind as possible, but will be useful when planning the offwind legs of your journey.

You work the above procedure in reverse
★ Estimate the expected tidal stream
★ Estimate your expected speed and, using the construction shown, work out the required course
★ Add a correction for leeway (upwind).

That is the basic principle of all the navigation required for coastal dinghy cruising; how much of it you actually put into practice depends on your patience and prevailing weather conditions.

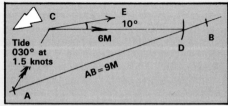

Establishing a course to steer from A to B, a distance of nine miles. With a boat speed of 3 knots and favourable tidal stream, the expected time is slightly more than two hours. Lay off two hours of tide from A to C, then strike off an arc representing two hours of boat speed. This crosses AB at point D, and so the direction of line CD gives the required course. Making allowance for 10° leeway gives a heading CE. Finally, the length of AD gives the actual distance covered in the two hours, from which an ETA at B can be established